PETER SIDWELL

SIMPLY GOOD BREAD

Publisher
Peter Sidwell / RMC Brainwave

Photography **Richard Faulks** Art Direction **Mik Baines** Text **Alan Air** Print **Simon & Schuster (UK)**

Good Taste 19 Portland Rd Keswick Cumbria CA12 5BS

Printed and bound in Italy by Rotolito Lombarda S.p.A.

SGB05

Welcome!

The success of my first book, *Simply Good Taste*, encouraged me to write *Simply Good Bread*.

It is packed with dozens of easy-to-make bread recipes to suit every mealtime and occasion – from a humble lunch or family picnic to a special dinner party.

As automatic breadmakers deliver great results with the minimum of effort, I asked Panasonic and Carrs Breadmaker to endorse the recipes in this book.

I hope you feel inspired to have a go at making lots of my favourite loaves.

Let me know how you get along!

Peter Sidwell

SGB**07**

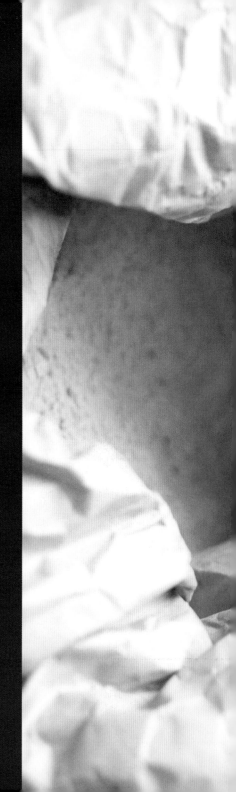

I always cook with the best kitchen equipment and the best local ingredients that I can afford. As my grandmother used to say – buy cheap, buy twice...

I use Carrs Breadmaker flour, not because it's produced near my home in the Lake District, but because it's the best you can buy.

Recently, I was lucky enough to tour the company's mill at Silloth on the west coast of Cumbria. Ships bring in the best wheat from around the world and a unique milling process turns it into the finest bread flour.

Similarly, I use a Panasonic breadmaker because it does everything I could ever want a breadmaker to do. It kneads, proves and bakes loaves to perfection.

Happy breadmaking!

Don't be fooled by the mill stones! I haven't got the time or the energy to grind my own flour but it made a great shot for the book

SGB**11**

Contents

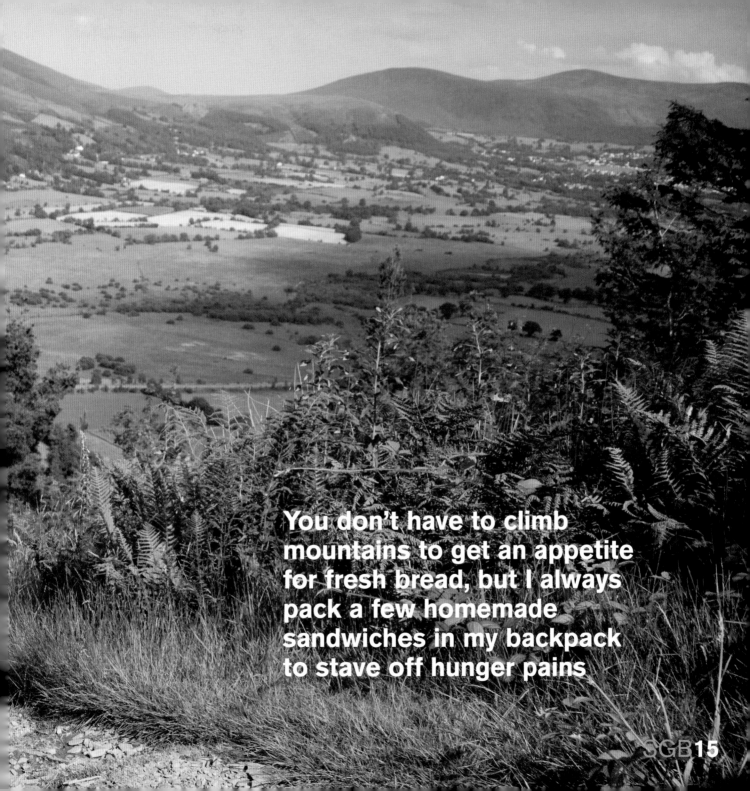

You don't have to climb mountains to get an appetite for fresh bread, but I always pack a few homemade sandwiches in my backpack to stave off hunger pains

Chapter one
BASIC
BREAD

SGB**17**

Back to basics

One of my favourite memories from boyhood is tearing into the house from a game of football and cutting myself a thick slice of homemade bread. Still warm from the oven, it tasted like nothing else on earth.

Twenty years on, *Simply Good Bread* celebrates my continuing love affair with this versatile food. Delicious, full of goodness and great fun to make, home-made bread should be at the heart of every household.

Never made bread before? Let me show you how. This section is your own personal toolkit, helping you to make and bake basic loaves.

From just three main ingredients – flour, yeast and water – you can make an array of amazing breads. Try a simple wholemeal loaf, batch of white rolls or healthy seeded bread.

Always use a good quality bread flour and let your breadmaker do the rest. When you are confident try a challenging ciabatta or flavoursome foccacia...

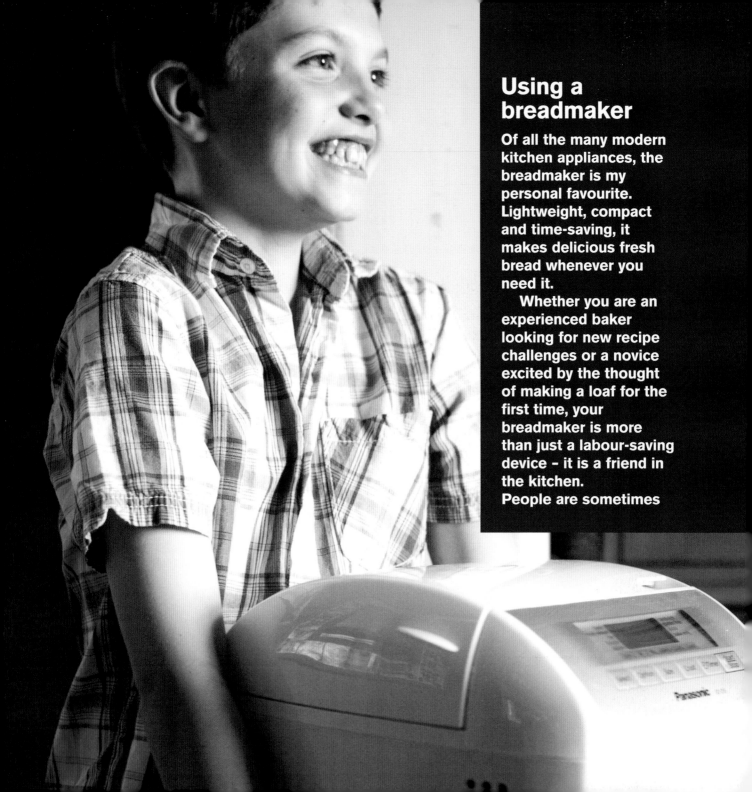

Using a breadmaker

Of all the many modern kitchen appliances, the breadmaker is my personal favourite. Lightweight, compact and time-saving, it makes delicious fresh bread whenever you need it.

Whether you are an experienced baker looking for new recipe challenges or a novice excited by the thought of making a loaf for the first time, your breadmaker is more than just a labour-saving device – it is a friend in the kitchen.

People are sometimes

surprised by just how easy it is to use a breadmaker – perhaps remembering school cookery classes and all the effort and time needed to make a loaf by hand!

But once you've decided on a recipe, simply put all your ingredients into the breadmaker, close the lid, press a couple of buttons and stand back and let it do all the work.

Yes, it really is that straightforward.

If your breadmaker has a timer you can set it to bake a loaf overnight, just in time for breakfast. Most breadmakers even have a dispenser for adding nuts, raisins or chocolate chips during cooking and they also allow you to select the size of loaf and type of crust.

After use, simply wipe down with a soft damp cloth, ready for the next loaf. Look after your breadmaker and it will keep you and your family in fresh bread for many years to come.

Making dough in a breadmaker

Some of the recipes in *Simply Good Bread* require you to make dough in your breadmaker. Don't panic! After putting your ingredients into the bread pan, simply press the 'dough' button and remove when ready. Then, follow my instructions for using the dough to create different types of loaves, before baking in a conventional oven or even on a barbecue.

Handling dough

Don't be afraid to handle dough – it's tactile, fun, versatile and therapeutic.

If your dough is too sticky simply dust your hands with a little flour. Relish the experience. Human beings have been handling dough for thousands of years.

It's the backbone of civilisation; from the Greeks and Romans to the present day.

SGB**23**

Basic instructions

To make a loaf in a breadmaker simply follow the manufacturers' instructions regarding the order of ingredients and set to bake.

When the bread is ready, remove immediately from the pan and allow to cool.

The following nine recipes are the 'basics' from which you can make almost every other type of bread in this book

Breadmaker recipes

WHITE

Setting
Basic/Normal

Yeast
1 tsp

Flour
White 500g

Salt
1.25 tsp

Sugar
1.5 tsp

Butter/Oil
25g

Water
340ml

ENRICHED

Setting
Basic/Normal

Yeast
1 tsp

Flour
White 500g

Salt
1 tsp

Sugar
25g

Butter/Oil
25g

Water
300ml

Egg
1 medium

BASIC WHITE DOUGH

Setting
Pizza/Dough

Yeast
1 tsp

Flour
White 500g

Salt
1.25 tsp

Sugar
1.5 tsp

Butter/Oil
25g

Water
300ml

Breadmaker recipes

BROWN

Setting
Basic/Normal

Yeast
1 tsp

Flour
Brown 500g

Salt
1.25 tsp

Sugar
1.5 tsp

Butter/Oil
25g

Water
340ml

50/50

Setting
Wholewheat

Yeast
1 tsp

Flour
Wholemeal 250g
White 250g

Salt
1.25 tsp

Sugar
1.5 tsp

Butter/Oil
25g

Water
360ml

WHOLEMEAL

Setting
Wholewheat

Yeast
1 tsp

Flour
Wholemeal 500g

Salt
1.25 tsp

Sugar
1.5 tsp

Butter/Oil
25g

Water
380ml

Breadmaker recipes

BAGUETTE

Setting
Pizza/Dough

Flour
White 125g
Overnight sponge 490g*

Salt
1 tsp

CIABATTA/FOCACCIA

Setting
Pizza/Dough

Flour
White 125g
Overnight sponge 490g

Salt
1 tsp

Butter/Oil
25g

NAAN

Setting
Pizza/Dough

Flour
White 225g
Overnight sponge 490g

Salt
1 tsp

Sugar
25g

Butter/Oil
25g

*To make an overnight sponge simply mix 250g strong white flour, 240ml water and 1 tsp yeast in a bowl. Cover with a tea towel secured with an elastic band and leave for 12 hours.

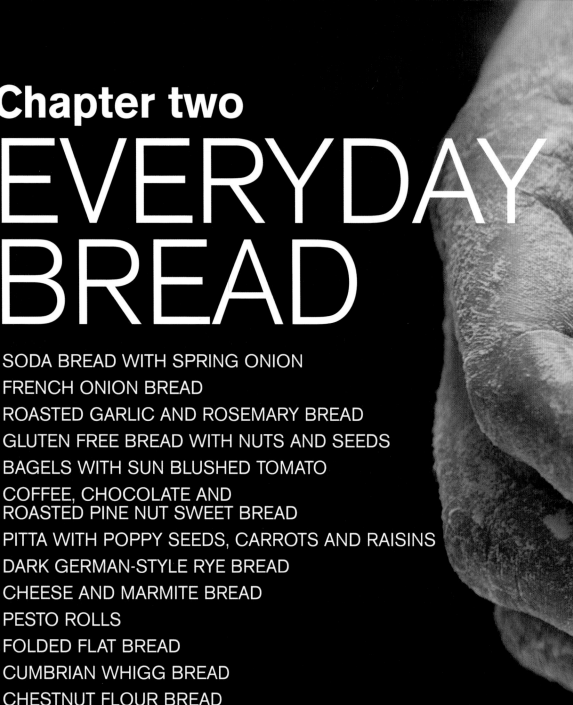

Chapter two
EVERYDAY BREAD

SGB**31**

Easy living

Over the last couple of years or so I've noticed that people are re-examining what is really important to them. The mad scramble to work harder and longer just to buy bigger, better houses and cars seems to be on the way out. Like fashion, lifestyles and attitudes often come full circle.

Baking your own bread – part of a gradual return to the essentials of life – breathes life into every nook and cranny of your home. Set the timer on your breadmaker so the aroma of freshly-baked bread wakes you up in the morning.

Hmm... warm bread, creamy butter and fresh coffee! What better way to start your day?

Whether you live in the countryside or middle of a large city it is easy to lose sight of the things that matter. Modern life is so demanding that it is all too easy to rush to the shop to grab a white sliced loaf without thinking.

Like intensively farmed chicken, mass produced bread can't hold a candle to a homemade loaf in terms of taste and nutrition. With breadmaker flour and an automatic breadmaker you can make a scrumptious loaf - like bread used to taste - in the time it takes you to drive to the shop.

Make everyday breads the backbone of your pantry - great for sandwiches, quick snacks and lighter meals.

SODA BREAD WITH SPRING ONION

MY NANA WAS IRISH AND I HAVE FOND MEMORIES OF HOLIDAYS IN BALLYMONEY WHERE SOME OF MY RELATIVES STILL LIVE. IRISH SODA BREAD IS SO EASY TO MAKE. NO PROVING, JUST MIX AND BAKE. IT'S THE PERFECT PARTNER TO IRISH STEW OR SOUP AND EVEN BETTER TOASTED THE NEXT DAY

Here's how...

Sieve flour, soda, salt and white pepper into a bowl.

Using a pair of scissors cut spring onions into the bowl using all of the onion, white and green.

Make a well in the middle and pour in the yogurt, oil and the milk.

Stir the mixture together and add more milk as required, to form a soft dough.

Place the dough into your parchment lined breadmaker and place on the bake only setting for 45 minutes.

Ingredients

450g self-raising flour
1 tsp bicarbonate of soda
1 tsp salt
$\frac{1}{4}$ tsp ground white pepper
1 bunch of spring onions
2 tbsp plain yogurt
50ml oil or melted butter
220ml milk

FRENCH ONION BREAD

I LOVE FRENCH FOOD SO IF YOU ARE MAKING THE
'KING OF SOUPS' JUST DOUBLE UP ON THE ONIONS,
GARLIC AND VEGETABLE STOCK FOR THIS HEARTY
BREAD ACCOMPANIMENT

Here's how...

Follow the manufacturers' instructions regarding the order of liquid/dry ingredients and set your machine to the dough/pizza setting.

Slice onion as thinly as possible and place into a medium-sized saucepan with the oil. Season the onion with salt and pepper (to draw the water out of the onions and help them caramelise quickly).

Crush the garlic clove and add to the onions along with the chopped thyme and cook gently until the onions turn golden (the more you cook them without burning the sweeter the onion flavour). Add the vegetable stock, reduce the volume by half, then leave the onions to cool.

Turn out the dough, press it out into a flat circle, spread with mustard and place a good spoonful of the onions into the centre. Bring all the edges of the dough together into the middle and press them together to seal the onions into the middle of the bread. Turn the bread dough over onto a lined baking tray. Using a pair of scissors cut a cross into the top of the bread and grate plenty of cheese on top.

Add a few springs of fresh thyme and prove in a warm place for 20-30 minutes.

Bake in a hot oven for 30-40 minutes at 200°C or until it is golden on top and sounds hollow on the underside when tapped.

Ingredients

Basic white dough
(made with 300ml
water) see p25
1 large white onion
1 tbsp vegetable oil
Salt and pepper
1 clove of garlic
1 tsp fresh thyme,
chopped
600ml vegetable stock
2 tbsp French mustard
100g Swiss Gruyère
cheese
Few sprigs fresh thyme

ROASTED GARLIC AND ROSEMARY BREAD

EVERYONE SHOULD HAVE ROOM FOR ROSEMARY IN THEIR GARDEN. A HEARTY, ROBUST HERB THAT CAN BEAR TOUGH BRITISH WINTERS, IT SUITS ALL MEDITERRANEAN TYPE FOOD. PERFECT WITH ROASTED GARLIC

Here's how...

Place the bulb of garlic into an oven proof dish with the olive oil.

Roast in the oven for an hour at 150°C until the garlic goes really soft and sweet. Remove the garlic from the oven and allow it to cool.

Follow the manufacturers' instructions regarding the order of liquid/dry ingredients and set your machine to the dough/pizza setting.

Turn out the dough and press it out into a flat round. Pull the garlic bulb apart and squeeze each clove out of its skin onto the dough. Strip off the rosemary leaves and sprinkle on top. Gently knead the dough, enough to incorporate the garlic and rosemary into the bread, taking care not to break up all the garlic as you want the cloves to stay as whole as possible.

Form the bread into a bloomer shape. Leave it to prove for about 30 minutes. Cook in a hot oven at 200°C for 20-25 minutes until golden and the loaf sounds hollow underneath when tapped.

Ingredients

Basic white dough (made with 300ml water) see p25
1 bulb of garlic
50ml olive oil
2 sprigs of fresh rosemary

GLUTEN-FREE BREAD
WITH NUTS AND SEEDS

GLUTEN-FREE BREAD IS A TOUGH CULINARY NUT TO CRACK AS
WITHOUT GLUTEN IT IS DIFFICULT TO HOLD THE AIR IN THE LOAF.
IT IS BEAUTIFUL EATEN FRESH BUT QUICKLY GOES ROCK HARD.
MY ADVICE IS TO BAKE IT, LET IT COOL, CUT INTO SLICES, FREEZE
AND TOAST FROM FROZEN

Here's how...

Before making the bread, roast the nuts and seeds to enhance their
nutty flavour. Sprinkle with a little salt and leave to cool. (I suggest you
buy a packet of each of the seeds and nuts, cook them all together
and when cooled store in an air tight container as they are great for
baking or stirring through salads to give texture and flavour.)

Place the water, vinegar, oil, eggs, salt and sugar into the bread pan.
Add the flour, seeds and yeast and set your breadmaker to the gluten
free setting with dark crust.

Ingredients

1 tbsp linseeds
1 tbsp pumpkin seeds
1 tbsp sesame seeds
1 tbsp millet seeds
1 tbsp walnuts, chopped
350ml water
1 tsp cider vinegar
4 tsp vegetable oil
2 medium eggs
1 tsp salt
1 tsp sugar or honey
450g gluten free flour
$1\frac{1}{2}$ tsp fast action/easy
blend yeast

BAGELS WITH SUN BLUSHED TOMATO, TOASTED (SERVED WITH CREAM CHEESE)

I LOVE THE TEXTURE OF BAGELS. NOWADAYS, THEY ARE MOBILE FOOD FOR THE CITY BEING CONVENIENT, VERSATILE AND PERFECT FOR ALL SORTS OF FILLINGS, OR TOASTED LIKE MINI PIZZAS. I CAN'T THINK OF A BETTER INGREDIENT COMBINATION THAN SUN BLUSHED TOMATOES AND CREAM CHEESE

Here's how...

Place all ingredients except the tomatoes into the bread pan by following your manufacturers' instructions regarding the order of liquid/dry ingredients. Place tomatoes in raisin/nut dispenser (if available) and set your machine to the basic raisin dough setting. If you do not have a nut/raisin dispenser, when the machine indicates (with a beeping sound), add the tomatoes.

When the cycle is complete, remove the dough. Punch down, cover and allow to rest for 10 minutes.

Divide dough into nine equal portions. Working quickly, shape each into a smooth ball. Punch a hole in the centre and pull gently to produce a 5cm hole. Place them on a large greased baking sheet. Cover and allow to prove for 20 minutes (start timing after first bagel is shaped).

Bring a large shallow pan of water to the boil and place 3-4 bagels in at a time. Cook for 1-2 minutes on each side then transfer them to a lined baking tray. Brush with an egg yolk wash, if desired, and bake in the oven for 20 minutes at 180°C.

Ingredients

1 tsp fast action/easy blend yeast
400g strong white flour
1 tsp of dried oregano
1 tsp salt
1 tbsp sugar
1 tbsp olive oil
220ml water
10 sun blushed tomatoes

COFFEE, CHOCOLATE AND ROASTED PINE NUT SWEET BREAD (PERFECT WITH COFFEE)

I LOVE CAFÉ CULTURE AND BUILT MY BUSINESS *GOOD TASTE* AROUND GREAT-TASTING COFFEE. I AM ALWAYS LOOKING OUT FOR THE ULTIMATE COMPANION FOR MY ESPRESSO, LATTE OR CAPPUCCINO. THIS BREAD COMES PRETTY CLOSE TO PERFECTION

Here's how...

Place the yeast in the bread pan followed by the flours, cocoa powder, salt, sugar, coffee, milk, egg and yolks, orange zest and butter and set your machine to the dough setting.

When the cycle is complete remove the dough from the bread pan and place on to a lightly floured surface. Knock it back gently, press the dough flat and sprinkle over the roasted pine nuts and the chocolate chunks. Fold the dough back into its self so the nuts and chocolate run through the dough evenly.

Shape and place in a round baking tin lined with parchment and leave to prove for at least 30 minutes or until it doubles in size.

Bake at 180°C for 30-40 minutes until it springs back when pressed.

Ingredients

1 tsp fast action/easy blend yeast
200g strong white flour
200g pasta flour
1 tsp cocoa powder
1/2 tsp salt
2/3 tbsp sugar
1 shot of good strong coffee (1 espresso or 2 tsp instant coffee dissolved in a splash of hot water)
140ml milk
1 egg
2 egg yolks
Zest of half an orange
75g butter at room temperature
50g roasted pine nuts (baked in an oven for 10 mins at 150°C until golden)
125g dark chocolate chunks

PITTA WITH POPPY SEEDS, CARROT AND RAISINS (SERVED WITH HOUMOUS)

PITTA BREADS ARE UNIVERSALLY POPULAR. USE THEM WITH DIPS TO START ANY PARTY OR MEAL – LET EVERYONE JUST TUCK IN. MY ONE-YEAR-OLD DAUGHTER LIKES TO DIP EVERYONE'S BREAD FOR THEM, ONLY THEN CAN THEY EAT! THIS IS A BASIC PITTA BUT I WANTED TO SHOW YOU ANOTHER USE AS A HEALTHY SANDWICH

Here's how...

Follow the manufacturers' instructions regarding the order of liquid/dry ingredients and set your machine to the dough/pizza setting.

Turn the dough onto a floured surface and divide into 12 pieces. Roll out the portions into oval pitta shapes, around $1/2$ cm thick. Bake the pitta on a lined baking tray at 200°C for about 5 –10 minutes (If the weather permits cook them on the barbecue grill – you'll get a fantastic colour and flavour.)

For the salad

Place the oil, honey and orange juice in a mixing bowl and whisk together lightly. Grate the carrots into the bowl over the dressing, add the raisins, poppy seeds and coriander and mix well to ensure the salad is dressed.

To serve

Cut each pitta bread in half and spread a little houmous. Fill with as much of the salad as you can!

Ingredients

Basic white dough (made with 300ml water and 2 tbsp olive oil) see p25
Houmous

Carrot salad

2 tbsp olive oil
2 tbsp honey
2 tbsp orange juice
4 washed and peeled carrots
50g raisins
2 tbsp poppy seeds
A few sprigs fresh coriander

DARK GERMAN-STYLE RYE BREAD

A SAVOURY BREAD WITH A DISTINCTIVE FLAVOUR.
AS GERMAN AS THE BLACK FOREST AND A GREAT
STARTER TOASTED AND SERVED WITH SMOKED
SALMON. THIS RECIPE IS AN ONGOING DEVELOPMENT
BETWEEN MYSELF AND DAN, ONE OF MY CHEFS WHO
SHARES MY PASSION FOR BAKING BREAD

Here's how...

Use the rye blade and follow the manufacturers'
instructions regarding the order of liquid/dry
ingredients and set your machine to the rye setting.

Ingredients

1 tsp fast action/easy
blend yeast
300g rye flour
200g strong wholemeal flour
2 tsp black treacle
1 tsp of salt
400ml water

CHEESE AND MARMITE BREAD

MARMITE IS MY DESERT ISLAND FOOD. I WAS FED IT AS A KID AND I TAKE A JAR WITH ME EVERYWHERE I GO. I PACK IT ALONG WITH MY PASSPORT. ON MY FIRST DATE WITH MY FUTURE WIFE I ASKED IF SHE LIKED MARMITE. SHE SAID YES SO I KNEW WE WOULD MAKE IT

Here's how...

Follow the manufacturers' instructions regarding the order of liquid/dry ingredients and set your machine to the dough/pizza setting.

Turn the dough onto a lightly floured surface and roll into a rectangle.

Spread the marmite on top and sprinkle with the cheese.

Roll the dough towards you to make a Swiss roll and place on parchment lined baking tray with the folded edge underneath.

Leave the dough to prove for about 30 minutes or until it doubles in size.

Bake it in a hot oven for about 25-30 minutes at 200°C or until golden and it sounds hollow underneath.

Ingredients

Basic white dough (made with 300ml water) see p25
2 tbsp Marmite
100g good quality English mature cheddar, grated

PESTO ROLLS

I SENT DAN, ONE OF MY CHEFS, TRAVELLING AROUND
ITALY SO HE WOULD GET MY PASSION FOR ITALIAN FOOD.
HE GOT IT! HE AND I DEVELOPED THIS TOGETHER AFTER
SEEING SOMETHING SIMILAR IN VENICE. SERVE AS AN
ALTERNATIVE TO GARLIC BREAD WHEN EATING PASTA
OR SWAP FOR A SANDWICH

Here's how...

Follow the manufacturers' instructions regarding the order of liquid/dry
ingredients and set your machine to the dough/pizza setting.

Turn the dough onto a lightly floured surface and roll into a rectangle
40 x 30cm.

Spread the pesto on the dough and roll it like a Swiss roll.

Cut the dough into 4cm slices and transfer onto a parchment lined
baking tray.

Sprinkle with a little sea salt and leave to prove for 20 minutes.

Bake in a hot oven about 200°C for 20 minutes until golden brown.

Ingredients

Basic white dough
(made with 300ml
water and 25ml olive
oil) see p25
4 tbsp pesto
Sea salt

FOLDED FLAT BREAD (SERVED WITH PUMPKIN AND MOZZARELLA CHEESE)

PUMPKIN ALWAYS REMINDS PEOPLE OF AN AMERICAN HALLOWEEN BUT ACTUALLY IT'S A POPULAR MEDITERRANEAN INGREDIENT. THE SWEET PULP IS A GREAT COMPLEMENT TO THE MOZZARELLA CHEESE

Here's how...

Slice the pumpkin into eight pieces, drizzle with olive oil, add a bulb of garlic and roast at 180°C for 40 minutes until tender. Leave to cool.

Follow the manufacturers' instructions regarding the order of liquid/dry ingredients and set your machine to the dough/pizza setting.

Turn the dough onto a lightly floured surface and cut into 8 pieces.

Roll out each portion into a circle about 10cm in diameter

Lay a strip of greaseproof paper over one side of each of the circles, fold the dough over the paper, place on a parchment lined baking tray and leave to prove for 20 minutes. Bake for 20 minutes at 180°C until golden brown.

Cut the pumpkin into slices; squeeze the garlic cloves out of their skins and spread onto the bread. Place the pumpkin and mozzarella slices into the flat bread together with a few dressed salad leaves.

Alternatively fill flatbread with air dried ham, capers and rocket leaves dressed with olive oil and a little lemon juice – another great combination!

Ingredients

Basic white dough (made with 300ml water) see p25

Filling

1 small pumpkin
1 tbsp olive oil
1 bulb garlic
1 mozzarella ball, sliced
Dressed salad leaves

CUMBRIAN WHIGG BREAD

I FIRST TASTED WHIGG BREAD AS A YOUNG BOY AT A CAFE IN HAWKSHEAD IN THE LAKE DISTRICT, WHICH HAS SINCE CLOSED DOWN. IT'S A DELICIOUS MILK BREAD AND BEAUTIFUL SERVED WITH A TOP-QUALITY STRAWBERRY OR RASPBERRY JAM

Here's how...

Follow the manufacturers' instruction regarding the order of liquid/dry ingredients and set your machine to the basic/normal setting, large loaf, medium crust.

Ingredients

Basic white bread
(made with 340ml milk)
see p25
1 tbsp caraway seeds

CHESTNUT FLOUR BREAD

I DISCOVERED CHESTNUT FLOUR ON MY TRAVELS THROUGH ITALY. IT GIVES BREAD A DELICIOUS SMOKY FLAVOUR AND IS LOWER IN GLUTEN. I HAVE ENJOYED IT MANY TIMES AT A TUSCAN MARKET. YOU CAN MAKE YOUR OWN CHESTNUT FLOUR BY WHIZZING ROASTED CHESTNUTS IN A FOOD PROCESSOR

Here's how...

Place all ingredients into the bread pan except the sultanas by following your manufacturers' instructions regarding the order of liquid/dry ingredients. Place sultanas in nut/raisin dispenser (if available) and set your machine to the basic/normal raisin setting, large loaf, medium crust.

If you do not have a nut/raisin dispenser add the sultanas and close the lid when the machine indicator sounds (usually a beep).

Alternatively, follow the manufacturers' instructions regarding the order of liquid/dry ingredients and set your machine to the dough/pizza setting. When cycle is complete, remove the dough from the machine. Punch down, cover and allow it to rest for 10 minutes.

Shape into a round and using scissors or a sharp knife score the top of the dough

Leave the dough to prove for about 30 minutes or until it doubles in size.

Bake the bread for about 25-30 minutes at 200°C or until golden and sounds hollow underneath.

Ingredients

1 tsp fast action/easy blend yeast
250g strong white flour
250g chestnut flour
1 tsp sugar
1 tsp salt
370ml water
75g sultanas

CORIANDER AND CUMIN BREAD

THESE TWO SPICES ARE THE BACKBONE OF AROMATIC ITALIAN COOKING AND THEY MAKE A TRULY TASTY BREAD. SERVE IT WITH CORONATION CHICKEN, INVENTED IN 1953 TO CELEBRATE ELIZABETH II ASCENDING THE THRONE

Here's how...
Follow the manufacturers' instructions regarding the order of liquid/dry ingredients and set your machine to the basic/normal setting, large loaf, medium crust.

Ingredients
Basic white bread
(made with 340ml water
and 30g of yogurt) see p25
1 tbsp cumin seeds
1 tbsp coriander seeds

Chapter three
ENTERTAINING

Share with friends

I love entertaining at home. What could be more exciting than sharing food with friends? I've never met anyone who doesn't love freshly-baked bread so I always serve it at a dinner party or special occasion.

It's great to tear and share or to plunge into dips or soups. Use spices, herbs and flavoured oils to turn everyday breads into mouth-watering bites.

Worried about slaving over dough whilst your guests are knocking at the door? Relax. Set your breadmaker to do all the hard work before they arrive.

Every dinner party needs an ice-breaker. Sometimes, the intoxicating aroma of freshly-baked bread is enough to get everyone talking before your guests have even taken off their coats.

I love it when friends invade the kitchen, drawn by the irresistible smell of a warm loaf.

If you want to impress your guests cook flatbreads in front of them, pour the wine and let the chatter and laughter flow.

PUMPKIN, WALNUT AND BLUE CHEESE BREAD

AUTUMN IS THE SEASON FOR PUMPKINS BUT SUBSTITUTE WITH ROASTED BUTTERNUT SQUASH AT OTHER TIMES OF THE YEAR. TASTY AND CRUNCHY, THIS BREAD IS GREAT TORN INTO CHUNKS AND SERVED WITH A HEARTY SOUP

Here's how...

Roast the pumpkin by cutting it into quarters or in half again depending on the size, season with salt, pepper and a little olive oil rubbing well into the flesh of the pumpkin.

Place it on a baking tray and roast at 200°C for 30 minutes until the flesh is tender. When it is cool enough to handle peel or cut the skin away and mash the sweet orange flesh with a folk or blend until smooth.

Place all ingredients together with the mashed pumpkin into the pan except the roasted walnuts by following your manufacturers' instructions regarding the order of liquid/dry ingredients.

Place walnuts in nut/raisin dispenser (if available) and set your machine to the basic/normal raisin setting, large loaf, medium crust. If you do not have a nut/raisin dispenser, when the machine indicates (with a beeping sound), add the toasted walnuts and close the lid.

Ingredients

100g pumpkin
1 tsp fast action/easy blend yeast
500g strong white flour
1 tsp sugar
1 tsp salt
$1/4$ tsp ground white pepper
300ml water
1 tsp olive oil
50g good local blue cheese
50g toasted walnuts

SESAME AND PRAWN BAGEL

A DELICIOUS BAGEL INSPIRED BY PRAWN TOAST WHICH
EVERYONE SEEMS TO LOVE. SERVE WITH CHOPPED
CORIANDER, SLICED SPRING ONIONS AND A SWEET
CHILLI DIPPING SAUCE

Here's how...

Follow the manufacturers' instructions regarding the order of
liquid/dry ingredients and set your machine to the dough/pizza
setting. When cycle is complete, remove dough from machine. Punch
it down, cover and allow the dough to rest for 10 minutes.

Divide the dough into eight portions. Working quickly, shape each into
a smooth ball and make a hole in centre pulling gently until the hole
is around 5cm. Place onto a large greased baking sheet. Cover and
allow them to rise for 20 minutes, starting to time after the first bagel
is shaped.

Bring a large shallow pan of water to the boil and place 3-4 bagels in
at a time, cooking for 1 minute on each side. Transfer to a lined
baking tray. Brush with egg yolk wash, if desired, and bake for 20
minutes at 180°C.

While the bagels are baking remove the tails from the prawns and
place them into a food processor. Blend with the egg yolks, five spice
and cream.

Remove the bagels from the oven, cut them in half and spread the
prawn mix onto the cut side. Dip the bagel prawn side down into the
sesame seeds and replace onto the baking tray.

Place the bagels into the oven at 160°C for approximately 8-10
minutes to cook the prawns through. (To check if the prawns are
cooked, press lightly. If firm to touch, they are done.)

Ingredients

1 tsp fast action/easy
blend yeast
400g strong white
flour
1 tbsp sugar
3/4 tsp salt
1 tbsp vegetable oil
250ml water

Topping

200g raw tiger prawns
2 egg yolks
1 tsp Chinese Five
Spice
2 tbsp double cream
4 tbsp sesame seeds

FLAT BREAD
(SERVED WITH TZATZIKI)

THIS RECIPE REMINDS ME OF THE DAY MY WIFE EMMA
AND I MOVED INTO OUR FIRST HOME, WHICH DID NOT
EVEN HAVE A KITCHEN OR OVEN. THAT NIGHT I JUST LIT
A BARBECUE, THREW ON FLAT BREADS, WHIPPED UP A
POT OF TZATZIKI AND CRACKED OPEN A FEW CHILLED
BEERS. THE UNPACKING HAD TO WAIT

Here's how...

Follow the manufacturers' instructions regarding the order of liquid/dry
ingredients and set your machine to the dough/pizza setting.

Whilst the dough is being made make the tzatziki by placing the yogurt
into a bowl, adding the dried mint and olive oil. Finely chop the fresh
mint, grate the garlic and add to the bowl, mixing well. Season to taste
and refrigerate.

When cycle is complete, remove dough from machine and place on a
floured work surface. Knead for about a minute then cut the dough into
around 10 pieces. Roll each ball out flat, about 1cm thick, and lay them
onto a plate between baking parchment paper.

The flatbreads can be cooked either in a frying pan or on a barbecue
grill – simply heat a dry frying pan and cook the breads for about
1-2 minutes on each side. When using a barbecue choose the coolest
place on the grill (usually at the sides) and cook the flatbreads for
1-2 minutes on each side. Serve with tzatziki.

Ingredients

Basic white dough
(made with 300ml
water and 1 tsp fresh
herbs e.g. rosemary,
thyme, parsley or
chives and 30ml extra
virgin olive oil) see p25

For the tzatziki

1 tub good quality
300g Greek yogurt
1 tsp dried mint
30ml extra virgin
olive oil
2 tbsp fresh mint
$^1/_2$ garlic clove
Salt and pepper

BREADSTICKS

BOUGHT BREAD STICKS ARE OFTEN DRY AND
TASTELESS. REFLECTING MY LOVE OF ITALIAN
CUISINE, THESE ARE FUN TO MAKE AND
ABSOLUTELY DELICIOUS

Here's how...

Follow the manufacturers' instructions regarding the order
of liquid/dry ingredients and set your machine to the
dough/pizza setting.

When the cycle is complete, scoop out the dough onto a
floured work surface and divide into two. Roll out the first
portion into a rectangle about $\frac{1}{2}$ cm thick. Top one half of
the dough with your chosen filling and fold over to encase
the contents. Roll the filled dough back into the original shape
and cut into strips about 2cm wide. Place on a lined baking
tray. Repeat with the second portion of dough. Experiment
by twisting the dough sticks before baking.

Brush the bread sticks with the beaten egg and bake in
the oven at 180°C for about 20 minutes until golden brown
and crisp.

Ingredients

1 tsp fast action/easy
blend yeast
500g strong white flour
1 tsp salt
1 tsp sugar
280ml water

For the fillings

Olive tapenade and
parmesan
Pesto
Sea salt and rosemary
Dijon mustard and
cheddar
1 beaten egg

NAAN WITH CUMIN AND BLACK ONION SEEDS

I WAS BROUGHT UP IN YORKSHIRE AND A 'LADS' NIGHT OUT'
USUALLY INVOLVED A CURRY, LOTS OF NAAN BREADS TO
MOP UP THE JUICES, AND A FEW BEERS. MOST OF US ARE
NOW MARRIED WITH YOUNG KIDS SO THIS RECIPE – SERVED
WITH A SPICY BALTI OR DANSAK – IS PERFECT FOR A 'LADS'
NIGHT IN' AND A FEW LESS BEERS

Here's how...

Toast the seeds in a dry frying pan until they start to crackle.

Follow the manufacturers' instructions regarding the order of liquid/dry ingredients, add the toasted seeds and set your machine to the dough/pizza setting.

When the cycle is complete, turn the dough out onto a floured work surface and knead the bread by hand for about a minute. Cut the dough into six portions and roll each portion into an oval about 1cm thick.

Either cook the naan in a dry frying pan on a low heat or pre-heat a baking tray and cook in the oven for approximately 10 minutes at 200°C.

Ingredients

1 tsp cumin seeds
1 tsp black onion seeds
1 tsp fast action/easy blend yeast
500g strong white flour
1 tsp salt
1 tsp sugar
50ml yogurt
280ml water

CIABATTA WITH BLACK OLIVES

AGAIN, THIS REFLECTS MY LOVE OF ITALIAN FOOD.
CIABATTA IS OFTEN SERVED WITH A GOOD PASTA DISH
BUT I PREFER TO JUST DIP IT INTO A HIGH-QUALITY
VIRGIN OLIVE OIL OR EQUALLY TASTY BALSAMIC VINEGAR

Here's how...

For the starter dough, mix the starter ingredients in a bowl, cover with a tea towel and secure with an elastic band. Leave for 12 hours to prove at room temperature.

To make the ciabatta place the proved starter dough into the pan and follow the manufacturers' instructions regarding the order of all the liquid/dry ingredients (but using just half the olive oil and omitting the olives at this stage) and set your machine to the dough/pizza setting. When cycle is complete, remove dough from machine and knead in the black olives. Place into a shallow dish with the other half of the oil, cover and allow to prove slowly for 3 hours.

Pre-heat the oven to 230°C. Place the ciabatta in the hot oven and reduce the temperature to 210°C. Bake for 25 minutes.

Ingredients

Starter
1 tsp fast action/easy blend yeast
500g strong white flour
480ml water

Ciabatta
500g Starter dough
50ml extra virgin olive oil
250g strong white bread flour, plus extra for dusting and kneading
40ml water
1½ tsp salt
1 tsp fast action/easy blend yeast
100g black olives, chopped

FENNEL AND SULTANA BREAD

I LOVE THE COMBINATION OF SULTANAS AND FENNEL.
THE ANISEED FLAVOUR OF THE FENNEL IS OFFSET BY
THE SWEETNESS OF THE DRIED FRUIT. ADD A LITTLE
RYE FLOUR TO GIVE IT AN EVEN RICHER FLAVOUR

Here's how...

Mix the starter ingredients in a bowl, cover with a tea towel and secure with an elastic band. Leave for 12 hours to prove at room temperature.

Place all ingredients together with the starter dough into the bread pan except the fennel seeds and sultanas by following your manufacturers' instructions regarding the order of liquid/dry ingredients. Place the fennel seeds and sultanas in nut/raisin dispenser (if available) and set your machine to the basic/normal raisin setting, large loaf, medium crust.

If you do not have a nut/raisin dispenser, when the machine indicates (with a beeping sound), add the fennel seeds and sultanas and close the lid.

Alternatively, follow the manufacturers' instructions regarding the order of liquid/dry ingredients, and set your machine to the dough/pizza setting. When cycle is complete, remove the dough from the machine. Punch down, cover and allow it to rest for 10 minutes.

Shape into a large ring. Leave the dough to prove for about 30 minutes or until it doubles in size.

Bake the bread for about 25-30minutes at 200°C or until golden and sounds hollow underneath

Ingredients

Starter
1 tsp fast action/easy blend yeast
500g strong white flour
480ml water

Dough
500g Starter dough
100ml water
250g dark rye flour, plus extra for dusting and kneading
1 1/2 tsp salt
1 tsp sugar
1 tsp fast action/easy blend yeast
2 tsp fennel seeds
75g plump sultanas

SWEET POTATO AND SMOKED PAPRIKA BREAD

THIS IS A WARMING BREAD AND GREAT FAVOURITE WITH MY CUSTOMERS – ESPECIALLY THOSE WHO HAVE JUST SPENT SEVERAL HOURS ON A WINTRY FELL IN THE LAKE DISTRICT! IT GOES DOWN A STORM SERVED WITH TOMATO AND GOATS' CHEESE SOUP OR A THICK WINTRY STEW

Here's how...

Bake the sweet potatoes in the oven at 190°C until soft, about 30-40 minutes. Remove skins and mash well.

Follow the manufacturers' instructions regarding the order of liquid/dry ingredients adding the sweet potato and paprika then set your machine to the basic/normal setting, large loaf, medium crust.

Ingredients

200g sweet potatoes
1 tsp fast action/easy blend yeast
500g strong white flour
1 tsp salt
1 tsp sugar
290ml water
1 tbsp smoked sweet paprika

CIDER APPLE BREAD

AN ENGLISH CLASSIC, PACKED WITH DISTINCTIVE
FLAVOURS. BRILLIANT FOR MAKING THICK-CUT
SANDWICHES STUFFED WITH ALMOST ANY FILLING YOU
CAN THINK OF. GREAT WITH CHEESE

Here's how...
Follow the manufacturers' instructions regarding the order
of liquid/dry ingredients and set your machine to the
basic/normal setting, large loaf, medium crust.

Ingredients
1 tsp fast action/easy
blend yeast
300g strong white flour
200g malted or
granary-type flour
1 tsp salt
1 tsp sugar
1 tsp ground white pepper
350ml dry cider
1 apple, grated
1 sprig rosemary, chopped

MUSTARD AND TARRAGON SWIRL

A FANTASTIC SAVOURY BREAD. INSTEAD OF ONE
LARGE LOAF, TRY BAKING INDIVIDUAL ROLLS INSIDE
NEW TERRACOTTA POTS – YES, THE SAME ONES YOU
BUY FROM THE GARDEN CENTRE

Here's how...

Follow the manufacturers' instructions regarding the order of
liquid/dry ingredients and set your machine to the dough/pizza
setting. When cycle is complete, remove dough from machine
and roll it into a sausage shape.

Using a pastry brush spread the mustard along the length of the
dough, sprinkle with tarragon, shape into a coil and transfer to a
lined baking tray.

Brush with the beaten egg yolk and sprinkle with mustard seeds
and a little sea salt, if desired.

Leave the bread to prove for an hour or until it doubles in size.
Bake for 45 minutes at 200°C until golden and crisp. To check
if it is cooked tap the underside of the bread and if it sounds
hollow it is done.

Ingredients

Basic white dough
(made with 300ml water
and without added fat)
see p25
3 tbsp Dijon mustard
1 tsp fresh tarragon,
chopped
1 beaten egg (yolk only)
1 tsp mustard seeds
(optional)
1 tsp sea salt (optional)

SUN-DRIED TOMATO AND THYME LOAF

SUN-DRIED TOMATOES ADD AN INTENSE FLAVOUR TO ANY DISH AND THIS BREAD IS NO EXCEPTION. PERFECT WITH ALMOST ANY MEDITERRANEAN DISH BUT I LIKE TO TOAST IT AND SPREAD WITH PESTO

Here's how...
Place all ingredients together into the pan, except the sun-dried tomatoes, by following your manufacturers' instructions regarding the order of dry/liquid ingredients.

Place sun-dried tomatoes in nut/raisin dispenser (if available) and set your machine to the basic/normal raisin setting, large loaf, light crust.

If you do not have a nut/raisin dispenser add the sun-dried tomatoes when the machine indicates (with a beeping sound) and close the lid.

Ingredients
Basic brown bread
(340ml water including the water from the soaked sun-dried tomatoes)
see p25
12 sun-dried tomatoes, soaked and chopped
2 tsp fresh thyme, chopped

CHORIZO AND BLACKENED CHILLI BREAD

TAPAS PLATTERS HAVE NEVER BEEN MORE POPULAR, PROBABLY PART OF THE TREND TOWARDS MORE INFORMAL WAYS OF EATING AND SOCIALISING. YOUR FRIENDS WILL FIGHT FOR A CHUNK OF THIS SHARP-TASTING BREAD

Here's how...

Blacken the chilli by placing it in aluminium foil and burning it in a flame from the hob. When the chilli is cool, dice it as finely as possible.

Place all ingredients except the chorizo into the bread pan by following your manufacturers' instructions regarding the order of liquid/dry ingredients. Place chorizo in nut/raisin dispenser (if available) and set your machine to the basic/normal raisin setting, large loaf, medium crust.

If you do not have a nut/raisin dispenser, when the machine indicates (with a beeping sound), add the chorizo and close the lid.

Ingredients

1 red chilli
Basic white bread
(made with 300ml water
and 30ml olive oil)
see p25
100g chorizo, diced

MOZZARELLA AND CHERRY TOMATO LOAF

FOR THIS LOAF I'VE SIMPLY COMBINED THE
INGREDIENTS FROM ONE OF THE MOST POPULAR
STARTERS IN ITALIAN RESTAURANTS THROUGHOUT
THE LAND. A GREAT DIPPING BREAD

Here's how...

Follow the manufacturers' instructions regarding the order of
liquid/dry ingredients and set your machine to the dough/pizza
setting. When cycle is complete, remove dough from machine
and roll it into a rectangle.

Scatter the tomatoes and mozzarella over the centre third of the
dough, tear up the basil leaves and add them to the tomatoes
and mozzarella.

Fold the bread over the filling twice so it encases the filling.

Transfer to a lined baking tray and leave to prove in a warm
place for approximately 40 minutes or until it doubles in size.

Bake in a hot oven about 200°C for 30 minutes until golden
brown.

Ingredients

Basic white dough
(made with 300ml water
and 30ml olive oil)
see p25
10 cherry tomatoes,
halved
1 mozzarella ball, sliced
1 handful of basil leaves

GOATS' CHEESE AND ROASTED RED PEPPER BREAD

TEAR 'N' SHARE BREADS ARE GREAT FOR PARTIES AND SUMMER BUFFETS IN THE GARDEN AND THIS RECIPE IS UNIVERSALLY POPULAR WITH MY FAMILY AND FRIENDS. INVARIABLY, ONE TRAY IS NEVER ENOUGH

Here's how...

Follow the manufacturers' instructions regarding the order of liquid/dry ingredients and set your machine to the dough/pizza setting.

Place the red pepper into the oven on a baking tray at 200°C for 20 minutes until soft then put it into a plastic bag and seal (or put into a bowl and cover it with cling film). This will cause the pepper to steam and separate the skin from the flesh. After 10 minutes remove the pepper from the bag, scrape off the skin and dice the flesh roughly into 1cm pieces.

When cycle is complete, remove dough from machine, turn it out of the bread pan onto a lightly floured work surface.

Roll the dough out into a 40cm x 30cm rectangle, spread evenly with the roasted red pepper and sprinkle with cheese. Roll the far side of the dough towards you to create a Swiss roll. Cut the dough into 3cm slices.

Line a 25cm cake tin with baking parchment, place the slices cut side down into the tin, brush with the egg yolk and leave to prove for 30-40 minutes.

As the dough proves it will expand and link all the portions together.

Bake at 220°C for 20-25 minutes or until golden brown.

Ingredients

1 red pepper
Basic white dough (made with 300 ml water and no added fat) see p25
100g goats' cheese, crumbled
1 beaten egg (yolk only)

Chapter four
OUTDOOR

SGB97

Eating al fresco

Bread, like all foods, tastes better outdoors – whether in the park with the kids, on top of a mountain or by a river with your mates or in the back garden with the neighbours. But there's a lot more to eating bread outside than simple sandwiches.

Try bagels, naans, pittas, tortillas and chapatis stuffed with cheeses, meats and healthy salad. I sometimes cook fresh pizzas topped with herbs from the garden in a wood oven outdoors. Truly delicious.

Bread is as magnificent and versatile as the British weather. Enjoy it – whether you are under an umbrella or a parasol!

One of the great things about making your own bread is that you choose exactly what goes into each recipe. Whether you're a serious athlete or just health-conscious, making your own bread gives you great control of your diet. Use less salt, more herbs, less butter, more yoghurt. Add superfoods – berries, nuts and seeds – for a fantastic energy boosting loaf.

Be inspired to try something different. Great health and great bread go hand-in-hand.

RYE WITH PECANS AND MILLET SEEDS

A NUTTY-FLAVOURED BREAD FULL OF ENERGY, FIBRE AND OMEGA 3 OILS TO POWER YOU THROUGH THE DAY. GREAT FOR ATHLETES AND THE HEALTH-CONSCIOUS

Here's how...

Roast pecans and millet seeds by spreading them out onto a baking tray, season with a little sea salt and a drizzle of olive oil and cook in the oven at 160°C for 10-15 minutes until golden and crispy.

Place all ingredients into the pan following your manufacturers' instructions regarding the order of liquid/dry ingredients and use the rye setting.

Ingredients

100g pecans
50g millet seeds
Sea salt
1 tsp olive oil
1 tsp fast action/easy blend yeast
300g rye flour
200g malty seeded flour
1 tsp sugar
1 tsp salt
370ml water

GINGERBREAD

AS A KID I LOVED GINGER NUT BISCUITS AND THIS
BREAD IS A NOSTALGIC NOD TO THE PAST. SPICY,
PUNGENT AND FULL OF THE FEEL-GOOD FACTOR
AND A TREAT FOR PICNICS

Here's how...

Melt the sugar, butter, syrup and treacle in a saucepan on a
low heat. Remove the paddle and line the bread pan up the
sides with silicone baking parchment.

Sift together the flour, ground ginger, baking powder,
bicarbonate of soda and the mixed spice into a bowl.

Make a well in the middle of the flour and pour in the mixture
from the saucepan.

Add the ginger beer, milk, egg and the candied ginger, mixing
until smooth and pour into the prepared bread pan.

Set the machine to bake only for 50 minutes. Test the bread
after about 40 minutes by pressing the top gently, if it springs
back it is cooked. If not then it will need longer.

Ingredients

100g muscovado sugar
75g butter
75g golden syrup
75g black treacle
225g plain flour
1 tsp ground ginger
1 1/2 tsp baking powder
1 1/2 tsp bicarbonate of
soda
1/2 tsp mixed spice
100ml ginger beer
50ml full fat milk
1 large egg, beaten
75g candied ginger,
chopped

JOHNNY CAKES

ALSO CALLED TWISTER AND DAMPER, THIS BREAD
ORIGINATES IN THE AUSTRALIAN OUTBACK. EVERY TIME
I COOK IT OUTDOORS PASSERS BY STOP TO HAVE A LOOK
AND A TASTE. A TRUE PEOPLE'S BREAD

Here's how...

In a bowl mix together the flour, salt and pepper and chopped tomatoes. Pour in the beer and bring the ingredients together using your hands. When the dough comes away from the bowl and is at a manageable consistency divide it into 10-12 portions and shape with a little flour.

When the barbecue is glowing and white place the Johnny cakes one at a time on the edge of the grill for about 2-3 minutes on each side so they puff up and are crisp on the outside.

You can also turn them into 'twisters' by rolling out thin strips, wrapping around a stick and cooking over an open fire for 2-3 minutes.

Ingredients

500g self raising flour
1 tsp salt
1 tsp ground white pepper
8 sun dried tomatoes, chopped
1x 300ml bottle of beer

MALT LOAF

MALT LOAF IS AN ICONIC PRODUCT AND A GREAT
FAVOURITE WITH PEOPLE ON THE COAST TO COAST
CYCLE ROUTE THAT PASSES THROUGH KESWICK
NEAR MY BISTRO

Here's how...

Place all ingredients into the pan except the sultanas and
follow the manufacturers' instructions regarding the order of
liquid/dry ingredients.

Place sultanas in the nut/raisin dispenser (if available) and set
your machine to the wholewheat raisin setting, medium loaf,
medium crust setting. If you do not have a nut/raisin
dispenser, when the machine indicates (with a beeping
sound), add the sultanas and close the lid.

Ingredients

1 tsp fast action/easy
blend yeast
200g strong wholemeal
flour
200g strong white flour
1tsp salt
1tsp sugar
1 tbsp molasses
1 tbsp black treacle
1 tbsp malt extract
75g butter
250ml water
200g sultanas

CHELSEA BUNS WITH SUPER FOODS

PACKED WITH ANTIOXIDANTS, THESE BUNS
ARE A TASTY WAY OF GETTING YOUR DAILY
QUOTA OF SUPER FOODS

Here's how...

Follow the manufacturers' instructions regarding the order of
liquid/dry ingredients and set your machine to the dough setting.

Place the dried fruit into a bowl, squeeze the lemon over the
top and leave it to soak while the dough is being prepared.

When cycle is complete, remove dough from machine, turn
it out of the bread pan on to a lightly floured work surface.

Using a rolling pin, roll the dough out into a 40cm x 30cm
rectangle, spread evenly with the dried fruit and sprinkle with
sugar. Roll the far side of the dough towards you to create
a Swiss roll. Cut the dough into 3cm slices.

Line a 25cm cake tin with baking parchment, place the slices
cut side down into tin, brush with the beaten egg yolk and leave
to prove for 30-40 minutes.

As the dough proves it will expand and link all the portions
together.

Bake at 220°C for 20-25 minutes or until golden brown.

Ingredients

1 tsp fast action/easy
blend yeast
500g malty seeded
flour
1 tsp sugar
1 tsp salt
320ml full fat milk
Zest of 1 lemon

Filling

100g dried sultanas
100g dried blueberries
100g dried cranberries
Juice of 1 lemon
100g sugar

1 beaten egg
(yolk only)

BANANA BREAD

RIPE BANANAS WORK BEST IN THIS DELICIOUS
BREAD THAT IS INCREDIBLY MORE-ISH AND
PACKED WITH INSTANT ENERGY

Here's how...

In a bowl cream together the butter and the sugar until it is
light and fluffy, add the beaten eggs, then the flour and
baking powder a little at a time until it is all incorporated.

Mash the bananas until smooth and stir into the mixture with
the yogurt. Add the nutmeg, sultanas and the roasted nuts
and poppy seeds and mix until smooth.

Spoon the mixture into the lined bread pan and set to bake
only for 1 hour. Test the bread after about 45 minutes by
pressing the top gently, if it springs back it is cooked. If not
then it will need longer.

Ingredients

100g butter
175g caster sugar
2 large eggs, beaten
200g self raising flour,
sifted
$1/2$ tsp baking powder
200g ripe bananas
85g yogurt
$1/2$ tsp nutmeg
125g plump sultanas
100g roasted walnuts
or pecans
50g poppy seeds

SGB**111**

BRAZIL NUT WHOLEMEAL BREAD

FIBRE IS LACKING IN MANY MODERN DIETS SO
A SLICE OR TWO OF THIS BREAD WILL BOOST
YOUR DAILY INTAKE. A SUBSTANTIAL BREAD
AND THE TREACLE GIVES IT BITE

Here's how...

Roast the Brazil nuts by placing them on a dry roasting tray or oven proof dish. Drizzle a little oil and salt over them and bake in the oven for 10 minutes at 150°C, until golden and crunchy.

Place all ingredients into the pan except the roasted Brazil nuts by following your manufacturers' instructions. Place Brazil nuts in nut/raisin dispenser (if available) and set your machine to the basic/normal raisin setting, large loaf, medium crust.

If you do not have a nut/raisin dispenser, when the machine indicates (with a beeping sound), add the Brazil nuts and close the lid.

Ingredients

75g chopped Brazil nuts
1 tsp olive oil
Salt
1 tsp fast action/easy blend yeast
250g strong white flour
200g strong wholemeal flour
50g muesli
1 tsp salt
25ml vegetable oil
25g black treacle or molasses
180ml water
180g yogurt

PRESSED FOCACCIA

THIS BREAD KNOWS HOW TO SURVIVE LIFE
IN THE FREEZER – WELL, THE REFRIGERATOR
ANYWAY. PERFECT FOR A PICNIC SERVED
WITH A GOOD SELECTION OF ANTIPASTI
FROM YOUR LOCAL DELI

Here's how...

Cut the focaccia in half and drizzle the cut side of the bread
with olive oil. Squeeze the garlic cloves out of their skins and
spread over the bread.

Scatter the cheese, basil and vegetables evenly over the
bread and top with the spinach leaves. Season with salt and
pepper and top with the other half of the focaccia.

Wrap the loaf in cling film and place a large dinner plate over
with something heavy to press it down. Leave the focaccia
overnight in the fridge to develop the flavours.

Ingredients

Focaccia
(see recipe p29)
30ml olive oil
6-8 roasted garlic cloves
200g ricotta cheese
12 basil leaves
100g roasted vegetables
2 handfuls baby spinach
leaves
Salt and pepper

Chapter five
FAMILY

SGB117

A family affair

Homemade bread is a kind of social glue. The family that makes bread together stays together? Something like that, I suppose.

I love spending time with my wife Emma, young daughter Poppy and her friends, tossing all sorts of ingredients into the breadmaker and throwing dough around the bread board. The look of wonderment on their faces as the finished bread comes out of the breadmaker is a joy.

Make breadmaking fun and the kids get a lesson for life. The first thing I ever made at primary school was cheese on toasted bread. Later, when I was 14, I made my first-ever bread in my cooking class. I loved handling the flour, working the dough, it was so tactile and I could see it rising in the bowl.

Afterwards, I threw the hot loaf in my rucksack and raced home shouting, 'Look what I've made?', and my mother found a squashed loaf nestling on a bed of crumbs!

We still laugh about my early breadmaking adventures to this day.

TOASTED OVEN BOTTOM MUFFINS

A DIFFERENT TAKE ON TRADITIONAL 'TOAST' THIS TASTY NORTHERN SNACK WILL BRIGHTEN UP A DULL SUNDAY AFTERNOON. THEY ARE EQUALLY SUITED TO SWEET AND SAVOURY SPREADS AND FILLINGS

Here's how...

Follow the manufacturers' instructions regarding the order of liquid/dry ingredients and set your machine to the dough/pizza setting. When cycle is complete, turn out the dough and place onto a floured work surface. Roll the dough out to about 3cm thick. Shape the muffins using a round cutter, re-rolling the excess dough to cut out the last few.

Heat a dry frying pan and place the muffins into the pan 4-6 at a time depending on the size of your frying pan. Cook the muffins on both sides until they are golden. Remove from pan and place them onto a tray. Bake in the oven at 180°C for a further 10 minutes.

Serve with fresh blueberries and lime zest/grated apple and cinnamon or cheese and roasted onions.

Ingredients

1 tsp fast action/easy blend yeast
500g strong white flour
1 tsp salt
1 tsp sugar
50ml yogurt
250ml milk

SIMPLE SOUR DOUGH

SOUR DOUGH IS THE HOLY GRAIL OF BREADS,
INCREASINGLY TRENDY TO SERVE BUT WITH
A PROVENANCE STRETCHING BACK IN TIME.
CRUSTY ON THE OUTSIDE, CHEWY IN THE
MIDDLE, I LOVE IT TOASTED AND SPREAD
WITH A BITTER ORANGE MARMALADE

Here's how...

For the sour starter

Mix the sour starter ingredients in a bowl, cover with a tea
towel and secure with an elastic band. Leave for 12 hours
to prove at room temperature. You will have enough starter
for two to three loaves. Keep in a refrigerator.

For the sourdough bread

Follow the manufacturers' instructions regarding the order
of liquid/dry ingredients and set your machine to the
French setting.

Ingredients

Sour starter

1 tsp fast action/easy
blend yeast
300g strong white flour
2 tbsp balsamic vinegar
300ml water
1 tsp sugar

Bread

250g sour starter
120ml water
250g strong white flour
1 tsp fast action/easy
blend yeast
1 tsp sugar
1 tsp salt

PIZZA AND CALZONE

A CLASSIC ITALIAN CREATION BURSTING WITH HEADY
AROMAS AND FRESH FLAVOURS

Here's how...

For the sauce

Halve the tomatoes, place on a baking tray and sprinkle them
with the salt, sugar, thyme and garlic. Drizzle with oil and vinegar
and place in the oven for 30 minutes at 160°C.

Leave to cool for a further 30 minutes. Either blend until smooth
in a food processor or press the tomato mix through a sieve.

For the pizza dough

Follow the manufacturers' instructions regarding the order of
liquid/dry ingredients and set your machine to the dough/pizza
setting. When cycle is complete, remove dough from machine
onto a floured work surface and divide the dough into 6 pieces.

Roll into circles about $1/2$ cm thick and spread a spoonful of the
tomato mixture onto the dough, top with sliced mozzarella and
torn basil leaves, and any other optional topping.

For calzone

Egg wash the edge of half of the circle of the dough, add your
chosen filling and fold over to make a semicircle. Press the edges
together by turning the dough over its self from left to right until
it is completely sealed.

Bake at 200°C for 12 minutes until golden brown.

Ingredients

Sauce
10 ripe tomatoes
2 tsp salt
2 tsp sugar
Fresh thyme
2 garlic cloves, crushed
1 tbsp olive oil
1 tbsp balsamic vinegar

Dough
1 tsp fast action/easy
blend yeast
250g strong white flour
250g pasta flour
1 tsp sugar
1 tsp salt
300ml water

Filling
2 mozzarella balls
10 fresh basil leaves
Olives, Parma ham,
roasted peppers,
anchovies... whatever
you fancy!

PRETZELS FOR KIDS

TOO MANY BAGS OF CRISPS ARE ONE OF THE DIETARY
REASONS OUR INCREASINGLY SEDENTARY CHILDREN
ARE PUTTING ON WEIGHT. THESE PRETZELS ARE EASY
TO MAKE AND KEEP WELL IN AN AIR-TIGHT CONTAINER

Here's how...

Follow the manufacturers' instructions regarding the order
of liquid/dry ingredients and set your machine to the
dough/pizza setting.

When cycle is complete, remove the dough from machine
onto a floured work surface and cut the dough into 25g balls.

Roll out the dough into long, thin strings, twist into pretzel
shapes and place on a baking tray. Bake at 150°C for 35-40
minutes. Cool and store in an air tight container.

Ingredients

1 tsp fast action/easy
blend yeast
500g strong white flour
1 tsp salt
1 tsp sugar
280ml water

HOLLOWED-OUT PLOUGHMANS

AN EYE-CATCHING AND ECO-FRIENDLY WAY OF SERVING THIS
TRADITIONAL DISH AS YOU EAT THE CONTAINER IT COMES IN

Here's how...

Follow the manufacturers' instructions regarding the order of liquid/dry
ingredients and set your machine to the wholewheat dough setting.

When cycle is complete, remove dough from machine onto a floured
work surface and knead the dough for several minutes. Shape into
a round loaf, place onto a lined baking tray and leave to prove for
30 minutes.

Bake in the oven for 30-40 minutes at 200°C. Check the bread is
cooked by tapping the underside. If it sounds hollow it's ready. Leave
to cool.

Cut the top off the loaf to make a lid and remove the soft crumb from
the inside to create a container. Don't throw away the inside of your
loaf as there are plenty of recipe ideas in the leftovers chapter.

Just before you are ready to go out fill the loaf with different cheeses,
meats, pickles/relishes and wrap with a tea towel.

Ingredients

1 tsp fast action/easy
blend yeast
300g malty seeded
flour
200g wholemeal flour
1 tsp salt
1 tsp sugar
340ml water
A selection of different
cheeses, meats and
local produce

SPRING ONION BAGEL (TOPPED WITH RAREBIT)

ENJOY THE ULTIMATE COMFORT FOOD WITH
A NICE MUG OF PIPING HOT TEA

Here's how...

Follow the manufacturers' instructions regarding the order of liquid/dry ingredients and set your machine to the pizza setting. When cycle is complete, remove dough from machine onto a lightly floured work surface and allow to rest.

Preheat the oven to 190°C. Bring a large saucepan of water to the boil, reduce heat to medium and simmer.

Divide the dough into nine even portions. Roll each portion into a ball. Push a lightly floured finger through the middle of the ball to create a hole pulling gently until the hole is around 5cm. Pat the ball gently to flatten. Place on the baking tray sprinkled with polenta, cover with oiled cling film and set aside for 10 minutes to rise. Remove cling film and add three of the bagels to the simmering water and cook for 1 minute. Use a slotted spoon to turn and cook for a further minute. Remove with slotted spoon and replace on the prepared baking tray. Repeat in two more batches with remaining bagels.

Whisk the egg white in a small bowl and brush evenly over each bagel and sprinkle with poppy seeds.

Bake in a preheated oven for 20-25 minutes or until golden brown. Cool on a wire rack.

Cut the bagels in half, cover in grated mature cheddar and Worcestershire sauce and place them under a hot grill until golden.

Ingredients

1 $\frac{1}{2}$ tsp fast action/ easy blend yeast
400g strong white bread flour
1 $\frac{1}{2}$ tsp salt
1 tbsp sugar
230ml warm water
4 spring onions, chopped

1 tbsp dried polenta
1 beaten egg (whites only)
1 tbsp poppy seeds
Grated mature cheddar
Worcestershire sauce

IRISH SODA FARLS

AGAIN REFLECTING MY ANCESTRY, THIS IS A QUICK
BREAKFAST DISH WHICH COMPLEMENTS GRILLED
PANCETTA, TOMATOES AND A POACHED FREE-RANGE EGG

Here's how...

Sieve the flour, soda, salt and pepper into a bowl. Make
a well in the middle and pour in the yogurt, oil and milk.

Stir the mixture together and add more milk, as required,
to form a dough.

Divide the mixture into two and roll out into flat 3-4cm thick
pancakes using the semolina or polenta to dust.

Preheat a dry frying pan.

Cut the farls into quarters and cook for three minutes on each
side until golden. Place them in the oven for 15 minutes at
180°C to finish cooking through.

Ingredients

450g self raising flour
1 tsp bicarbonate of
soda
1 tsp salt
$^1/_2$ tsp ground white
pepper
2 tbsp yogurt
50ml vegetable oil
220ml milk
50g ground semolina
or polenta

BRIOCHE FILLED WITH NUTELLA AND ROASTED HAZELNUTS

MY TAKE ON PAIN AU CHOCOLAT, THIS ENRICHED, SWEETENED BREAD DOUGH IS DELICIOUS WITH A GOOD-QUALITY VANILLA ICE CREAM. DO NOT EAT STRAIGHT FROM THE OVEN AS THE CHOCOLATE WILL BE REALLY HOT

Here's how...

Follow the manufacturers' instructions regarding the order of liquid/dry ingredients and set your machine to the basic dough setting.

When cycle is complete, remove dough from machine onto a lightly floured work surface and knead the dough for one minute. Divide into 10 portions. Roll out each piece into a circle and place a spoonful of Nutella into the centre along with six roasted hazelnuts. Bring all the sides of the dough together and press them to create a seal.

Place the rolls sealed side down on a lined baking tray and leave to prove for 30 minutes and bake in the oven at 190°C for 20-30 minutes or until golden brown.

Ingredients

1 tsp fast action/easy blend yeast
400g strong white flour
$1/2$ tsp salt
3 tbsp caster sugar
4 large eggs
125g butter
30ml milk
8 tbsp Nutella
50g hazelnuts

PARMESAN ROLLS

I LIKE TO SERVE THESE BREADS FILLED WITH A LOCAL
DRY CURED HAM AND SOME DRESSED ROCKET LEAVES.
SIMPLE, UNPRETENTIOUS FOOD

Here's how...

Follow the manufacturers' instructions regarding the order
of liquid/dry ingredients and set your machine to the
dough/pizza setting.

When cycle is complete, remove dough from machine onto
a lightly floured work surface and roll the dough out into
a rectangle about 1cm thick.

Grate the parmesan evenly over the dough.

Egg wash the long side nearest you and roll the dough from
the back towards you to make a Swiss roll. Cut the dough
into 4cm pieces and place them cut side down onto a lined
baking tray.

Brush with the beaten egg yolk and leave to prove for
20 minutes or until they have doubled in size.

Bake in the oven for 20 minutes at 200°C until golden brown.

Ingredients

Basic white dough
(made with 300ml
water) see p25
100g parmesan cheese
2 beaten eggs (yolks only)

Chapter six
LEFTOVERS

SGB139

Waste not, want not

**At last our throwaway society is in retreat.
More and more of us are throwing less and
less away. Never discard two-day old bread
that has gone slightly hard.**

Toast it for crostinis, make croutons for soup
or salads or dip slices into beaten egg and fry!
A classic bread and butter pudding takes no
time at all.

   Still got some hard crusts left over? Take the kids
to the local park and help them feed the ducks.
An old loaf packed with seeds will even be good
for the birds.

   I love collecting cooking and baking tips. I never
usually write them down but prefer to simply
remember them in my head.

   This final section breaks the habit of a lifetime! It is
full of handy hints and advice on how to get terrific
results. Through trial and error and listening to other
bakers I have discovered how to get the best out of
bread. I am delighted to pass them on.

Crumbs!

I never use shop-bought breadcrumbs; they are expensive and alien to my way of working in the kitchen. Homemade breadcrumbs are easy-to-make, improve the taste of many dishes and are cheap. Store in a re-sealable plastic bag in the freezer and use as required.

Follow these simple tips for perfect breadcrumbs:

Use any type of bread and even combine different types for some wonderful taste experiences.

Never use stale bread or you will get horrible stale-tasting breadcrumbs. Use dry bread for perfect results.

If your bread is too fresh and moist bake fresh bread slices in a slow oven for a few minutes.

Save spare bread slices and ends of bread in a large re-sealable plastic bag in the freezer until you have enough to make your breadcrumbs.

To make breadcrumbs place pieces of bread in a food processor and whizz until you reach a coarse mix. For finer crumbs in the future it is easy to give them another quick blast.

POOR MAN'S PARMESAN

WHEN YOU FANCY A TASTY QUICK PASTA DISH AND
THERE'S NO PARMESAN OR INGREDIENTS FOR SAUCE
DON'T DESPAIR. THIS RESCUE RECIPE WILL CHANGE
THE WAY YOU EAT PASTA - GUARANTEED

Here's how...

Put a large pan of salted water on to boil. Add the pasta
and cook for approximately 9-12minutes.

Place the breadcrumbs, chilli, anchovies and garlic into a
food processor and blend to a fine crumb.

Pour the olive oil into a frying pan and cook the breadcrumb
mixture on a gentle heat until golden and crispy.

When the pasta is cooked to taste, drain but retain some of
the cooking water as the starch helps the consistency of the
finished sauce.

Put the drained pasta back into the cooking pan with a little
of the retained cooking water. Add a generous splash of extra
virgin olive oil, sprinkle with the crispy breadcrumbs and serve
with a good twist of black pepper.

Ingredients
Serves 2

150g good quality pasta
4 tbsp fine breadcrumbs
1 small red chilli, deseeded
and finely chopped
2 tinned anchovies,
chopped
2 cloves garlic, finely
chopped
2 tbsp extra virgin olive oil
Freshly ground black
pepper

APPLE STRUDEL TOASTIE

I ALWAYS ENSURE THAT I HAVE SOME LEFTOVER
BRIOCHE TO MAKE THIS FANTASTIC, SIMPLE TOASTIE.
NOT AS AUSTRIAN AS THE HABSBURGS BUT
DELICIOUS NONETHELESS

Here's how...

In a bowl mix together the apple sauce, sultanas, mixed spice, sugar and lemon zest.

Spread one side of each slice of brioche with butter and turn them over, butter side down.

Spoon the spiced mixture onto one slice of the bread and place the other slice on top butter side up.

Preheat the grill or a toasted sandwich maker and when it reaches the right temperature place the sandwich in to toast.

Serve with some good ice cream or clotted cream.

Ingredients
Serves 1

2 tbsp apple sauce
1 tbsp sultanas
$1/2$ tsp mixed spice
$1/2$ tsp brown sugar
A few shavings of lemon zest
2 slices of leftover brioche
20g butter

CINNAMON TOAST
THIS SWEET TOAST IS PERFECT SERVED WITH
BARBECUED PLUMS OR A GOOD PLUM COMPOTE

Here's how...

Break the eggs into a bowl, add the sugar and cinnamon
and whisk together.

Cut the vanilla pod lengthways and using a knife scrape the
inside of the pod to release the vanilla seeds and add them
to the bowl, mixing well.

Heat a dry frying pan and add the butter.

Dip the bread into the sweetened egg mixture, ensuring that
the slices are well coated.

Place the bread into the frying pan and cook on each side
for 3-4 minutes or until golden.

Ingredients

Serves 1

2 large free range eggs
1 tbsp icing sugar
1 tsp of ground cinnamon
$1/2$ vanilla pod
50g butter
2 slices leftover white
bread

HERB-CRUSTED SALMON

BREADCRUMBS, HERBS, SALMON – HERB-CRUSTED
SALMON IT IS! AN ABUNDANT TASTY FISH, THIS RECIPE
IS A PERENNIAL FAVOURITE IN MY HOUSEHOLD

Here's how...

Preheat the oven to 180°C.

Place the chopped fresh herbs, salt, pepper lemon zest,
breadcrumbs and butter into a food processor and pulse
to mix.

Scoop the mixture out onto a piece of baking parchment or
cling film and press the mixture down. Place another piece
of parchment over the top and roll out the mixture to about
$1/2$ cm thick. Peel off the top layer of parchment revealing an
even crust.

Place the salmon fillets skin side up onto the crust. Cut
around the fish, lift them off the parchment and transfer
to a baking tray placing the fillets skin side down.

Bake the salmon in the preheated oven for approximately
12 minutes until the crust is golden.

Ingredients

Serves 2

25g mixed fresh herbs
(rosemary, chervil, basil),
chopped
Salt and pepper, to taste
Zest one lemon
100g breadcrumbs
75g butter
2 x 225g fresh salmon
fillets

CHORIZO SALAD

THIS SALAD DOESN'T LAST LONG AT THE TABLE IN
MY HOUSE. MEATY AND SATISFYING

Here's how...

Chop the chorizo and the ciabatta into chunks and place in
a roasting tray, drizzle with a little olive oil and place in the
oven for 40 minutes at 150°C until the croutons are crisp.

Leave the tray to cool to room temperature.

Roughly chop the coriander, core the lettuce, cut into quarters
and add to the croutons, mixing well. Transfer into a large
salad bowl.

In a measuring jug whisk together the vinegar and olive oil
to taste, pour over the salad and serve.

Ingredients
Serves 4

300g chorizo
$^1/_2$ ciabatta
1 handful of coriander
3 baby Gem lettuce
30ml sherry vinegar
90ml extra virgin
olive oil

THE ULTIMATE TOASTIE

JUST LIKE SKIING IS THE ULTIMATE SPORTING HIGH FOR ME, THIS TAKE ON A GREAT SANDWICH IS THE ULTIMATE TOASTIE. I ALWAYS MAKE IT ON MY ANNUAL SKI TRIP TO FRANCE

Here's how...

Butter the bread and turn it over, butter side down.

Lay a slice of dry cured ham on each slice of bread.

Spread the mustard on one slice and mascarpone on the other.

Season to taste with black pepper and a few sprigs of thyme.

Sandwich the bread butter side out and place into a dry frying pan on a low heat. Cook on each side for approximately 5 minutes or until the toastie is golden on both sides.

Ingredients

Serves 1

2 slices of leftover white bread
30g butter
2 slices dry cured ham
1 tsp Dijon mustard
1 tbsp mascarpone
Black pepper, to taste
2 sprigs thyme

PARMESAN-CRUSTED CHICKEN

SERVED WITH SLOW ROASTED VINE TOMATOES,
THE CONTRASTING FLAVOURS AND TEXTURE ARE
SIMPLY SUPERB

Here's how...

Season the chicken fillets on both sides with a little salt and pepper.

Lightly beat the eggs together with the milk.

Dust each chicken breast escalope in flour, dip into the beaten eggs and finally coat with the breadcrumbs mixed with the parmesan.

Fry the escalopes in a little hot olive oil until golden brown, about two minutes on each side.

Drain the cooked chicken on kitchen paper, then remove to a baking tray and cook for a further 12 minutes at 180°C.

Ingredients
Serves 4

4 chicken breasts,
boned, skinned and
pounded until 1cm thick
2 beaten eggs
1 tablespoon milk
60g plain flour
200g breadcrumbs
50g grated parmesan
Olive oil
Sea salt and freshly
ground black pepper

EGG BANGO

THIS RECIPE WAS INSPIRED BY A FRIEND OF MINE WHO
I FIRST SAW MAKING IT WITH ONE HAND IN A SLING
AFTER BREAKING HIS COLLAR BONE ON A SKI TRIP. I
USED BOTH MY HANDS TO MAKE THIS BUT IMAGINE
HOW HARD IT WOULD BE TO MAKE THIS WITH JUST
ONE FUNCTIONING ARM

Here's how...

Butter the bread on both sides and place under a preheated
grill toasting on both sides.

Heat the oil in a frying pan and cook the egg gently, to taste.

Place the egg between the toasted slices and season with
black pepper.

Ingredients

Serves 1

2 slices of leftover
white bread
30g butter
2 tbsp oil
1 free range egg
Black pepper

HONEY AND LAVENDER TART

A GREAT USE OF LAVENDER THAT WORKS PARTICULARLY
WELL WITH SWEET HONEY. MY WIFE EMMA ALWAYS DRIES
A FEW BAGS OF LAVENDER TO USE IN THE KITCHEN

Here's how...

Prepare the pastry by sifting the flour and icing sugar into a bowl.
Use your fingertips to rub in the butter until the mixture resembles
fine breadcrumbs.

Add the egg and mix well to form a dough and chill in the refrigerator
for 30 minutes. Preheat the oven to 180°C.

Roll the pastry dough out to 2mm thick and use to line a 20cm
tart ring.

Fill with baking beans and blind bake in the oven for 15 minutes, or
until the pastry is golden brown, removing the beans during the last
five minutes of baking. Allow to cool. Reduce the oven temperature
to 160°C.

Place the bread and the lavender into a food processor and pulse
to fine breadcrumbs.

Heat the butter in a pan until browned. Gently warm the golden syrup,
honey, lemon juice and zest in a pan and stir in the browned butter.

Mix the egg and cream until well combined. Pour the golden syrup
mixture into the combined eggs and cream and stir in the prepared
breadcrumbs.

Pour the mixture into the cooked tart case and bake in the oven at
160°C for 25 minutes. Turn the oven temperature down to 140°C and
bake for a further 20 minutes, or until the tart is golden brown and
bubbling. Remove from the oven and allow it to cool before turning out.

Ingredients

Serves 8

For the pastry

250g plain flour, plus
extra for dusting
50g icing sugar
125g chilled butter, cut
into cubes
1 free range egg,
lightly beaten

For the filling

90g leftover bread
1 tsp dried lavender
50g butter
250g golden syrup
100g local honey
1 lemon, zest and juice
1 large free range egg
40ml double cream

SALSA VERDE

A SUPERIOR ALTERNATIVE TO TRADITIONAL MINT SAUCE.
I THINK IT WORKS BETTER AS IT CUTS THROUGH THE
RICHNESS OF THE LAMB

Here's how...

Finely chop the red onion and garlic and place in a bowl with the mustard, vinegar and olive oil.

Add the chopped herbs and season to taste with salt and pepper.

Add the bread and leave to stand for 20 minutes, allowing the bread to soak up all the flavours. Taste, adding the sugar if desired.

Serve with roast lamb. Use any leftovers to add a zing to tomato salads or sandwiches.

Ingredients

Makes 1 jar

$1/2$ red onion
$1/4$ clove of garlic
1 tsp Dijon mustard
4 tbsp red wine vinegar
8 tbsp olive oil
2 large handfuls of mint, chopped
1 handful of parsley, chopped
1 slice of leftover white bread, cubed
1 tsp sugar (optional)
Salt and pepper, to taste

PANZANELLA SALAD

LOTS OF MY FAVOURITE MEDITERRANEAN INGREDIENTS
COMBINE TO PRODUCE A HEAVENLY SALAD THAT
EVERYONE LOVES

Here's how...

Pre-heat oven to 200°C.

In a large bowl, toss the bread with the olive oil, salt, pepper and garlic. Lay the seasoned bread on a baking sheet, and toast in the preheated oven until golden, about 5-10 minutes; allow to cool slightly.

Chop the peppers into chunks, drizzle with a little olive oil, salt and pepper and place on a preheated grill pan for 5 minutes until you get some really nice grill marks.

While the bread is in the oven, whisk together the olive oil and balsamic vinegar. Gently toss together the bread, tomatoes, onion, basil, olives and peppers. Toss with the vinaigrette and allow to stand for 20 minutes before serving. You might like to add a handful of toasted pine nuts before taking to the table?

Ingredients

Serves 4

300g leftover bread, torn into bite-size pieces
80ml olive oil
3 cloves garlic, finely chopped
1 red pepper
1 yellow pepper
60ml olive oil
30ml red wine vinegar
500g ripe cherry tomatoes, cut into wedges
125g sliced red onion
10 basil leaves, shredded
75g pitted and halved green olives
30g pine nuts, toasted
Salt and pepper, to taste

DUCK BREAD
A GREAT FAVOURITE WITH THE UBIQUITOUS MALLARD
DUCK THAT FREQUENTS CITY PONDS AND PARKS

Here's how...
Remove stale, unwanted bread from bread bin.

Place into reusable carrier bag.

Walk to the local park, children in tow.

Break into small pieces and toss to the ducks.

Smile and think how good life is...

Ingredients
Any unwanted bread, but loaves containing seeds are particularly good

Conversions

Oven Temperatures

°C	°F	Gas Mark	Oven
140	275	1	Cool
150	300	2	
170	325	3	Moderate
180	350	4	
190	375	5	Moderately Hot
200	400	6	
220	425	7	Hot
230	450	8	
240	475	9	Very Hot

Liquid Measurements

5ml	1 teaspoon (tsp)
10ml	1 dessertspoon (dsp)
15ml	1 tablespoon (tbsp) or $\frac{1}{2}$ fl oz
30ml	1 fl oz
60ml	2 fl oz
75ml	$2\frac{1}{2}$ fl oz
100ml	$3\frac{1}{2}$ fl oz
150ml	5 fl oz ($\frac{1}{2}$ pt)
300ml	$\frac{1}{2}$ pt
450ml	$\frac{3}{4}$ pt
600ml	1 pt (20 fl oz)
1 litre	$1\frac{3}{4}$ pt

Weights

15g	$\frac{1}{2}$ oz
25g	1 oz
50g	2 oz
75g	3 oz
110g	4 oz ($\frac{1}{4}$ lb)
150g	5 oz
175g	6 oz
200g	7 oz
225g	8 oz ($\frac{1}{2}$ lb)
250g	9 oz
275g	10 oz
300g	11 oz
350g	12 oz ($\frac{3}{4}$ lb)
375g	13 oz
400g	14 oz
425g	15 oz
450g	16 oz (1 lb)
500g	1 lb 2 oz
675g	22 oz ($1\frac{1}{2}$ lb)
1 kg	2.2 lb

NB Cooking times for fan assisted ovens may be shorter. Please refer to manufacturers guidelines.

All conversions are approximate

Be inspired to try something different. Great health and great bread go hand-in-hand

Acknowledgements

I would like to thank my fantastic wife Emma and beautiful daughter Poppy for their love and support. Without them I would not be able to achieve half of what I set out to do.

Thanks also to all my parents and in-laws for all their ongoing help and encouragement.

A special thank you goes to my fantastic team at Good Taste – Kylie Overton, Dan Grimshaw, Danny Hartley, Becca Newton, Ali Burlington and Edoardo Gren – who have all helped in their own special ways to make sure I was able to commit the time and energy to this book.

Thanks also to my friends James, Fiona and Jack Breedon for the loan of their kitchen.

Finally, I am grateful to Panasonic for their guidance in helping me to the get the best out of automatic breadmakers, and also to Carr's Flour for their generous donations of excellent flour!

Peter Sidwell

Bread is as magnificent and versatile as the British weather. Enjoy it - whether you are under an umbrella or a parasol!

Notes

Notes